SPELLING
REPAIR KIT

How to improve your ~~Speling~~ spelling skills

SPELLING
REPAIR KIT

To the fabulous Elis Stanley Vandyck. Elis has one "l", Vandyck is all one word and d-y-c-k, and fabulous is as fabulous does.
With tons of love, Dad

For John with affection and gratitude
Angela

CONTENTS

INTRODUCTION

Why not to buy this book

There are two reasons which people give for not bothering to learn to spell properly. They usually say either something like:

1. You don't really need to know how to spell.

> *So long as you get close,*
> *people know what you mean*
> *— and anyway all computers*
> *have spellchecks, these days, innit?*

OR

2. You can't learn how to spell.

> *You either can or you can't.*
> *Luckily I was born a brilliant speller.*

There are just two things to remember about these two points.

THEY ARE BIG FAT LIES.

Big Fat Lie One: "You don't really need to know how to spell".

This really is rubbish.
Question: Do you want to look **STUPID** ?
No, we didn't think so. Well, here are two facts then.

Remember, they're just facts, OK? Just accept it.

And we can prove it.

Look. Imagine you're an examiner, or an employer, or a friend reading one of these notes. Which one makes you think the writer is stupid?

I left my home in 1997 to do great things

I left ~~me~~ mi ~~home~~ hom in 19~~x~~97 ~~x~~ to do grate ~~thing~~ things

Clue: It's this one

If you've got a computer, you might think the spellcheck would solve all your problems – but you'd be wrong!

Spellchecks can only correct words if they're very nearly right anyway. And they can't pick out wrong spellings which would be right spellings if you meant something else. So, if you wrote "pane" (of glass) when you meant "pain" (in the . . . neck), it wouldn't correct you. It wouldn't pick up the "grate" in the note above. And anyway, if you haven't learnt to spell, what do you do when you haven't got the computer readily available. Look

STUPID ?

And if you thought spelling didn't matter, or that spellchecks would spot all mistakes, look:

You
are invited to
come
hunting bear.

You
are invited to
come
hunting bare.

The spellcheck wouldn't have picked that out, would it?

And you might think the difference mattered just a teeny bit, no?

Big Fat Lie Two: "You can't learn how to spell".

This really is rubbish, too. Again, we can prove it. This time, we can prove it through completely independent research.

We took fifteen people and one 1-week old baby called Elis. We set them all *exactly* the same spelling test, so that there was no unfairness.

The lad Elis didn't come first. Can you guess the reason why?

The *only* reason for this is - obviously - that Elis had not by the time of this test had a chance to learn how to spell.

See?

It's not just that you *can* learn how to spell - you *have* to. It's the only way.

Now, there's some good news. And some better news. And then some best news.

The GOOD news

is that in order to spell, you don't have to learn a dictionary. It's all a bit bewildering when you think of how many words there are (at the last count, absolutely tons). But the thing is, if you remember a few tricks (or "rules"), you'll be able to spell an enormous number of words.

So you don't have to be like:

Una the Unnecessary Worker

You can be like:

Stanley Savenergy

And now . . .

The BETTER news.

General Malaise

We'll muck about a bit along the way. So, watch this space:

Okay, you can stop watching the space now. Carry on.

For example, for no reason at all we're suddenly going to write:

The VEST.

Oh, all right, there is a bit of a reason for it. The word "vest" sounds like "best". And the best news is yet to come. PTO. (That is not POT misspelt. Or TOP misspelt. Or even TPO misspelt. It means "Please Turn Over".)

11

The BEST news is that you won't have to battle through this alone. You're going to be helped by the garage mechanics, who are:

Say hello, Zelda:

Hi.

I may be dull, but I summarise things clearly and in a concise way.

Say hello, (Dull) Colin:

Hat.

Say hello, Steven The Stupid Monster:

Oh dear. See if you can work out how Steven got his name.

There'll be a few other people dropping in along the way, too. But right now, let's go to work.

MORE THAN ONE

What's wrong with this note?

GIVE ME ALL YOUR BOXS OF SWEETES OR I'LL SMACK YOU IN YOUR TOOTHS WITH WET CODS

Well, for a start it's not very polite, is it?

But more importantly it looks very stupid because the spelling is all wrong for the plurals.

> A plural is a word which refers to more than one thing. So, the plural of "pen" is "pens".

Now, yes, it can be quite tricky making some nouns plural. There are some words that, frankly, act a bit weird when they go from singular (one) to plural. We're just about to have a look at those.

> A noun is a word that names —"identifies"— a thing, like car, spanner, repair, or terror!

But don't despair.

There is some slightly good news coming.

And then, there is some tremendously fabulous better news.

Hang on in there.

OK, here are some of the weird words.

Singular	Plural
one mouse	three mice
one tooth	five teeth
one woman	six women
one child	two children
one goose	four geese

Loopy. Mad. Sorry.

Then some words are weird because they don't change at all. They're exactly the same in the singular and in the plural.

one sheep	two sheep
one moose	five moose
one cod	three cod

Some words go to the other extreme and have *two* plurals.

appendix	appendixes
	appendices
memorandum	memorandums
	memoranda
syllabus	syllabuses
	syllabi

You should use your dictionary to check exceptional words like these and if you want to learn them you have to learn each word individually.

The slightly good news is that you probably know a lot of them already. And the fabulous news is that you do not need to learn the plural of every word you know!

Hundreds of thousands of words follow easy rules (or patterns). All you have to do with these straightforward words is to learn the rules they follow, and then you can spell huge numbers of words correctly.

A (one) sheep.   Two Sheep.   A sheep one-two.

Mr Clevertrousers' Advanced Mental Wandering for Curious Fools

Remember, you do not need to remember anything in this box - even this bit.

Some words have weird endings because of Latin. They're Latin words, and people just sort of got so into the habit of using the Latin version of the plural that they forgot to stop doing it when we started speaking English. You will come across some words that end in -um, for which the Latin plural was -a. More than one memorandum? They'd say memoranda.

Now, some people will tell you that Latin is terribly important, educates your mind, blah blah blah.

Well, if it's so cool, how come the people who go on about it are so boring, eh?

And remember –

syllabuses (the areas covered by courses or exams) should on no account be confused with the dreaded:

 silly buses.

Some of the rules you probably half-know already. You've just got to be confident enough to use them safely every time.

Take these two words, **chair** and **box**, for instance.

one chair   three chairs
one box   two boxes

How do you know whether to add –*s* or –*es* without having to learn each word individually?

There's a very easy answer.

You can always HEAR when you have to add -es because you are adding an extra syllable.

Say to yourself:
chair   chairs
box   boxes.

Can you HEAR the extra syllable when you say "box-es"?

Here are some words to say aloud. Count the syllables as you say them.

punch   punches
witch   witches
bus   buses

And look, it works for words which start with more than one syllable, too.

actress   actresses
princess   princesses   no extra syllable - not es!
witness   witnesses
elephant   elephants

You can see that if you add -es to a word of one syllable, you end up with two syllables. If you add -es to a word of two syllables, you end up with three syllables, and so on.

You've now learned two important spelling rules.

Syllable. Syllable. Hmm. Is that a type of pudding?

No, are you thinking of "syllabub", a dish made of cream or milk curdled with wine or similar, and sometimes solidified with gelatin?

Er, no, I remember which pudding I was thinking of... treacle tart.

Right. Well, the number of syllables in a word is the number of sounds in that word. So, "hat" has one syllable. "Thumps" has one but "punches" has two. "Zelda" has two. "Steven" has two, too.

Like this.

No, Steven, that's "Steven has a tutu". What I'm saying is that the word "Steven" has two syllables. But not, it seems, two brain cells. Let's see if anyone can do better than Steven. Can you say how many syllables there are in these?

Towns
Catapult
Pointy
"Help me, I'm stuck," said the man with the pointy head who had landed upside down.

Answers: 1, 3, 2, 19.

Remember now:

"Trou - ser"

2 Syllables.   2 Silly bulls[1].

No worries!   Worry...

[1] And now you know another difference between silly bull**s** and silly bus**es**. Clever, eh?

Rule 1

You make most words plural by adding **-s**.

Rule 2

You make some words plural by adding **-es** when you can *hear* that you need an extra syllable.

Why not simply say that words ending in sibilants require **-es** in the plural?

Well, yes. That's another way of putting it but then I'd have to explain that sibilants are hissing sounds like -s, -x, -z, -ch, -tch, and -sh. I will if you like. There, I've done it.

Now everyone can be clevertrousers.

Rule 2   **Pointlessly clever version.**

Words ending in sibilants require -es in the plural

which are hissing sounds like -s,-x,-ch, -tch and -sh

It's time for an MOT! (That's a **M**iserable **O**ld **T**est.) Test your understanding of these two rules by completing the following:

BASIC MOT

1. one book   two book____
2. one wish   three wish____
3. one teacher   four teacher____
4. one pen   five pen____
5. one glass   six glass____

The answers for all the tests are at the back of the book. Check yours before going on to the advanced MOT. Make sure that you understand exactly when you need to add -es and when you need just to add -s.

The advanced MOT may look hard because you may not have met all of the words before. Don't worry if any words are unfamiliar. We've deliberately put some hard words in to prove to you that you can apply the rules with absolute confidence and get the right answer every time.

ADVANCED MOT

1. winch____
2. ruminant____
3. blemish____
4. mnemonic____
5. zygoranismagicianisticalist_____ – see, you can
                                        even do it for
                                        words that
                                        don't exist.

Next we're going to look at how to form the plural of nouns ending in -y, like fairy, boy and party. Now, the important thing to remember is that it all depends on whether the word ends in a *vowel* + y, or a *consonant* + y.

What's a VOWEL?
What's a CONSONANT?

A, E, I, O, U are vowels. The rest of the letters of the alphabet are consonants.

Here comes Rule 3. It's wonderful because there are no exceptions at all. All the nouns in the English language which end in -y follow this rule.

Rule 3 Add **-s** to words ending in a vowel + y. Change y to i and add **-es** with words ending in a consonant + y.

Have a look at some examples.

examples of vowel + y

boy	boys
chimney	chimneys
monkey	monkeys
alley	alleys
day	days
guy	guys

examples of consonant + y

city	cities
party	parties
fairy	fairies
gipsy	gipsies
estuary	estuaries

Those vowels in full: **A E I O U**

Here's one way of remembering that the vowels are AEIOU.
Think of this picture and remember:

"An Entertaining Idiot Often Undresses"

Would you like to check *your* skills now? You will do just as well if you follow the rule carefully. In fact, if you follow the rule carefully, you *can't* make a mistake.

Just look at the last two letters. You have to know whether the word ends with a vowel + y or a consonant + y.

BASIC MOT

Make these words plural.

1. fly
2. toy
3. bully
4. holiday
5. donkey

6. berry
7. spy
8. story
9. valley
10. pony

I like rules which don't have any exceptions. I hope there are no exceptions to the next rule as well.

There are a few but nothing to worry about. You just have to say the words aloud and you'll know how to spell them.

Are you ready for the advanced MOT now? We've chosen long words that you may not know just to make the test look very difficult. As you know, you've just got to see whether the word ends in a vowel + y or a consonant + y to know how to form the plural correctly every time.

ADVANCED MOT

Make these words plural.

1. essay
2. fantasy
3. opportunity
4. factory
5. volley

6. university
7. quality
8. pulley
9. responsibility
10. convoy

Find out how well you did by checking your answers with the answers at the end of the book.

Y? Y? Y? Y?

What a very y-s little owl you are.

The next rule applies to nouns ending in -f and -fe.

Rule 4 Add **-s** to form the plural of words ending in **-f** or **-fe**.

In just a few words the f changes to v or ve in the plural. You can always HEAR when this happens: cal**ves**, hal**ves**, wi**ves**, li**ves**, thie**ves**, lea**ves**, and so on.

You don't need a sheaf of paper - use your loaf!   *You don't need sheaves of paper - use your loaves!*

So, what's the plural of "The White Cliff of Dover"?

Well, say the plural of "cliff" to yourself. It keeps the "f" sound, doesn't it? So, the plural of "cliff" is "cliffs".

And look how stupid you'd look if you wrote the wrong thing:

A. The White Cliffs of Dover.   **B. The White Clives of Dover.**

There's just one more rule we have to consider and that's the one for forming the plural of nouns ending in **-o**.

Before you turn the page, how many words can you think of that end in -o?

ODD ONE OUT

Which is the ONE word in this list which has a **v** sound in the plural?

giraffe
café
sheriff
shelf
cliff

Say them aloud and you'll hear the answer...

The answer is at the end of the book.

The Importance of Spelling Through the Ages, part 247

What is the plural of "wife"?

It was always very important to be able to show the difference between:

The Six Wives of Henry VIII

and

The Six Whiffs of Henry VIII.

Words ending in o

Here are some:

piano   banjo   soprano   contralto   photo
disco   rodeo   sombrero   cuckoo   kangaroo.

Rule 5

Add **-s** to form the plural of words ending in -o.

(No exceptionos, I hope!)

Just listen carefully.

There are just a few exceptions. That's why we've left this rule to the last in this chapter. There are two ways of tackling the exceptions. Choose whichever method suits you best.

Method 1: Use a dictionary. If you have to add -es in the plural because the word is an exception to the rule, the dictionary will remind you. If you just have to add -s, the dictionary won't bother to mention it.

Method 2: Learn the most important exceptions (the words that you're most likely to need) and just check the ones you're not certain about.

Learn: **cargoes   dominoes   echoes   heroes   mosquitoes**
potatoes   tomatoes   tornadoes   torpedoes   volcanoes

Perhaps you'd like to practise all that you have learned and
FIND THE MYSTERY WORD.

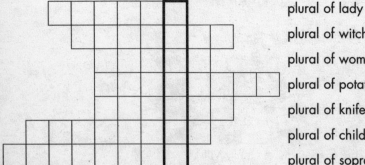

plural of lady

plural of witch

plural of woman

plural of potato

plural of knife

plural of child

plural of soprano

Just Mucking About

Do you know about palindromes?

A PALINDROME is a word or sentence that is the same spelled backwards. Like these:

Anna.

Hannah.

Pup, pip, pop, pip, pup.

Eve.

Madam, I'm Adam.

Was it a cat I saw?

How about this – siht tuoba woh.

Can you think of any? Do remember not to confuse:

1. a palindrome: **Eve**

with

2. a pally dromedary!

Will you be my friend?

COLIN'S CHALKBOARD CONCLUSIONS

PLURALS

1. Generally add -s.
2. Add -es if you can hear the extra syllable (eg boxes).
3. If a word ends vowel + y change the y to i and add -es. eg city, cities.
4. For words ending -f or -fe, change the -f or -fe to -v or -ve if you can hear that's what happens.
5. There are exceptions, including some mad ones. Try to learn the most common ones.

So, if you had me and <u>another</u> Colin here, Zelda, what would you say?

I'm twice as bored by you.

ADDING ENDINGS

Normally there's no problem when you add an ending to one word to make another one. You just join the ending on and that's that.

clean + **er** = cleaner
paint + **ing** = painting
play + **ful** = playful
astonish + **ment** = astonishment
trouble + **some** = troublesome
special + **ity** = speciality

Why not call these things by their proper name? They're suffixes. Everyone knows that!

CLEVER TROUSERS

It really doesn't matter whether you call them endings or suffixes.

I can give you a wonderful tip. Whenever you add "full" to a word, it ALWAYS becomes -ful.

Now that's what I call a use**ful** comment. I hope our boast**ful** friend is playing care**ful** attention to your help**ful** advice, Zelda.

Our next rule is about adding endings to -y words. It's the ones ending in a consonant + y that need special care.

Rule 6

Just add the ending if the word ends in a vowel + y.

play + ful = playful
play + ing = playing

BUT

Take care if the word ends in a consonant + y.
Change the y to i before adding the ending.

beauty + ful = beautiful
copy + ed = copied

(But keep the y before -ing: copying.)

SUPPLY THE VITAL MISSING LETTER!

1. enjoy + ment = enjo _ ment
2. cry + ed   = cr _ ed
3. pay + ing   = pa _ ing
4. early + er   = earl _ er
5. empty + ness = empt _ ness

Don't forget the exceptions -
said, paid, laid, and daily.

SOPHIE
SMARTIPANTS

Are you ready to try the advanced MOT?

Just remember:

play + ful = playful
beauty + ful = beautiful.

These will help you
to remember the rule.

We have deliberately tried to make the advanced MOT look very hard by putting in some words that you may never have tried to spell before. Just apply the rule and you'll supply the correct missing letter every time.

ADVANCED MOT

(It's not so difficult as it looks!)

Supply the vital missing letter:

1.	lonely + ness	=	lonel _ ness
2.	mercy + ful	=	merc _ ful
3.	portray + al	=	portra _ al
4.	melody + ous	=	melod _ ous
5.	annoy + ance	=	anno _ ance
6.	envy + able	=	env _ able
7.	employ + er	=	emplo _ er
8.	marry + age	=	marr _ age
9.	luxury + ous	=	luxur _ ous
10.	pity + less	=	pit _ less

Our next rule concerns words ending in silent -**e**.

You may already have had some problems with these words, wondering whether to keep the -e or drop it when you add an ending.

The secret is this:

Check whether the ending is a vowel suffix (an ending beginning with a, e, i, o, u, for example "ing") or a consonant suffix (an ending beginning with a consonant, for example "ful").

Rule 7

Drop the -e when you add a vowel suffix.
(Mak**e** + ing = ma<u>ki</u>ng)

Keep the -e when you add a consonant suffix.
(Car**e** + ful = ca<u>ref</u>ul)

Remember that -y counts as a vowel suffix when it sounds like -e: scare + y = scary.

It's worth learning five exceptions to the silent -e rule: truly, awful, ninth, argument, wisdom. You'd expect these words to keep the -e and they don't.

Sophie Smartypants has made three mistakes in her homework (hooray!). Be her teacher and mark her answers for her and write in the corrections for her to learn.

I.	love + ing	loving
2.	care + less	carless
3.	laze + y	lazy
4.	sincere + ly	sincerly
5.	safe + ty	saftey

As a result of being careless, I am now carless

Henry VIII needs help adding endings to silent -e words. He has been too lazy (laze + y) to learn the rule in the past. Now he's written a letter to Jane Seymour and needs help with five words. Could you look at this list and write the words he needs in the right spaces?

definite + ly   lone + ly   grate + ful
write + ing   hope + ing   sincere + ly

Dear Jane,

    I am _____ because I am so _____ since Anne Boleyn's head came clean off. Both my hired killers (Og and Stig) agree that it was _____ an accident. Or "Axe"-ident, more like, heh heh heh.

    Anyway, I was _____ you might be free next week. Or n-axe-d week says Stig. Heh heh. I would be _____ for a prompt reply.

                    Yours _____,
                    Henry VIII

PS: PBAAxe.

Now let's look at the 1-1-1 rule. This rule tells you whether you've got to double a letter or not.

First of all, try to guess why the rule is called 1-1-1.

Find *three* ways in which these words are alike.

fit   spot   sin   drop   flat

Could you find the three ways?

1.   They are all words of ONE syllable.
2.   They all end with just ONE consonant.
3.   They all have ONE vowel in the middle.

Calling it the 1-1-1 rule helps to remind you that the word has to fit the rule in three ways.

REMEMBER the rule does NOT apply to a word like **crash** because this ends in *two* consonants.

REMEMBER the rule does NOT apply to a word like **cool** because that has *two* vowels in the middle.

Now let's see what happens when you add vowel suffixes and consonant suffixes to 1-1-1 words.

Better still, see if you can work out the rule for yourself.

fit + ness = fitness   fit + est = fittest
spot + less = spotless   spot + ed = spotted
sin + ful = sinful   sin + er = sinner
drop + let = droplet   drop + ing = dropping
flat + ly = flatly   flat + en = flatten

Could you work out the rule?

Rule 8

NO CHANGE to a 1-1-1 word if you add a consonant suffix.
DOUBLE the last letter of a 1-1-1 word if you add a vowel suffix.

There's only one 1-1-1 rule
One 1-1-1 rule
And it's "No change to a 1-1-1 word for consonant suffixes, but double the last letter for vowel suffixes".

Which is the right spelling of the following not-at-all well known sayings?

1. The weather today will be hot and funy/funny.

2. Survival of the fatest/fattest.

Answers: funny, fattest

COLIN'S CHALKBOARD CONCLUSIONS

ADDING AN ENDING

1. Full is always 'ful' as an ending.
2. *i* Vowel + y – add the ending
   (but said, paid, laid, daily).
   ii Consonant + y – change y to i before adding
   the ending.
3. If a word ends in a silent -e:
   i drop it for a vowel suffix (treating y as a
   vowel here) eg make + ing = making.
   ii keep it for a consonant suffix
   eg care + ful = careful.
4. No change to a 1 – 1 – 1 word for consonant
   suffixes; double the last letter for vowel suffixes.

Ahhh, I like happy endings.

What, like
"And then Colin
got strung up"?

36

HOMOPHONES

Do you know what a homophone is? Homophones are groups of words which *sound* the same but which are spelled differently.

Here are some examples of homophones. You may know a lot of others.

blue and **blew**
weak and **week**
rain, **rein** and **reign**
pour, **paw** and **pore**

"Homophone" means same sound: homo (same) + phone (sound). More old language.

It is important to choose the right word for the situation because otherwise you risk confusing your reader.

For example, do you think this jar of face cream is going to be a big seller?

I meant for anyone except Steven.

There are hundreds of homophones in the English language. Most of them cause no trouble at all once you've got used to them. Some are more tricky.

Test how many you know in the puzzles that follow.

MISSING PARTNERS

Spell the missing partner. The first one has been done for you.

four	f o r
hole	_ _ _ _ _
tail	_ _ _ _
throne	_ _ _ _ _ _
wood	_ _ _ _ _
sun	_ _ _

Now use your answers to complete this newspaper item:

Bob's _____ was _____ out of school ___ eating the _____ school's food by himself. He told some _____ about getting into the Guinness Book of Records, but then he _____ , wouldn't he?

This section is very difficult. See how many missing partners you know.

prophet	_ _ _ _ _ _
aisle	_ _ _ _
medal	_ _ _ _ _ _
him	_ _ _ _
ceiling	_ _ _ _ _ _

IT IS OF COURSE IMPORTANT TO BE ABLE TO WRITE THE DIFFERENCE BETWEEN:

BRIGHTER THAN A THOUSAND SUNS

AND

BRIGHTER THAN A THOUSAND SONS.

MISSING PAIRS

Use these clues to find the missing pairs. The first one has been done for you.

a small hole that allows water to run out	l e a k
a vegetable belonging to the onion family	l e e k
opposite of female	_ _ _ _
letters and parcels sent through the post	_ _ _ _
to come to the end of life	_ _ _
to colour clothes permanently	_ _ _
the back part of the foot	_ _ _ _
to become cured	_ _ _ _
to change	_ _ _ _ _
the table used in church for the Communion service	_ _ _ _ _

Dictionary Quiz

Use your dictionary (if you wish) to find out the difference in meaning between these pairs.

serial	cereal	berth	birth
stationery	stationary	yoke	yolk
border	boarder		

Cereal Killer

Zandra has written a nice friendly letter to Percy but she has chosen the wrong homophone *ten times*. Can you spot the mistakes?

7 Seaview Road,
Brightling,
Devon.

Monday, 10th June

Deer Percy,

Wood yew like to come to stay with us for a hole weak? We can go to the beech every day and have a grate time.

Please right back soon and say yes.

With love,
Zandra

P.S. I hope yew can reed this!

MISSING LETTERS

Can you find the homophone and fill in the missing letters?

soul	s o l e
horse	h _ _ _ _ e
sum	s _ _ e
meet	m _ _ t
aloud	a _ _ _ _ _ d
check	c _ _ _ _ e

Next follows a checklist of everyday homophones that cause a lot of trouble. The examples should help you always choose the right word when you need it.

CHECKLIST

hear Can you **hear** that noise?
here Stay **here** and wait a moment.
it's **It's** been raining all day. (= it has)
its **Its** tail is twitching.
its **It's** alive! (= it is).
knew I **knew** your old grandmother.
new I prefer the **new** one.
know I **know** your girlfriend.
no I have **no** idea why she is called "Psycho".
passed She has **passed** her exam.
past They walked straight **past** us.
  The **past** is over and done with.
  Do you know the **past** tense of "go"?

their **Their** cat is missing.
there I'll wait for you over **there**.
they're **They're** coming home today.
  (= they are)
to We are going **to** Dublin.
  I'd like **to** help you.
too He is **too** lazy. (= excessively)
  Are you coming **too**? (= as well)
two You can have **two** cakes each. (= 2)
who's **Who's** been eating my sweets? (= who has)
who's **Who's** coming with me? (= who is)
whose **Whose** grandmother is this?
  The people **whose** cat is missing are very upset.

Hear, Pussycat!

Hear what?

TESTING, TESTING

Use the checklist to help you choose the
missing words in these sentences.

1. _____ coming to your party? (who's/whose)
2. I can _____ every word you say. (hear/here)
3. My cat is ___ lazy ___ catch more than ___ mice. (to/too/two)
4. _____ very windy today. (it's/its)
5. I _____ the answer. It's ___. (know/no)

OK, that's enough of that! Let's have a look at another group of
words that can cause a lot of trouble.

WORDS EASILY CONFUSED

These words are not homophones. They don't sound exactly alike but are close enough for people to muddle them up.

Make sure you know how to say them.

Make sure you know which is which.

TRICKY WORDS

bought (from BUY)
brought (from BRING)

I've **bought** you an ice-cream.
I **brought** my spider to school.

breath (rhymes with DEATH)

You can see your **breath** in the air on a cold day.

breathe (rhymes with SNEEZE)

"**Breathe** regularly," says top doctor.

clothes (you wear these)
cloths (do housework with these)

All my **clothes** are too small.
Use soft **cloths** to polish your furniture.

desert (very sandy!)

She was lost in the Sahara **desert** for three days.

dessert (pudding)

We had apple pie for **dessert**.

lightening (making lighter)

We are **lightening** her load as much as we can.

lightning (and thunder)

A loud clap of thunder followed the flash of **lightning**.

loose (not fixed tight)
lose (to stop having)

I have a **loose** tooth.
Don't **lose** this £5 note.

of (sounds like ov)

Would you like a piece **of** cake?

off (hear the F sound)

The thief ran **off**.

quiet (not noisy)
quite (absolutely)

She was as **quiet** as a mouse.
Are you **quite** sure you came from Mars?

were (rhymes with HER)
where (rhymes with AIR)

You **were** standing next to her.
Where you going?

TEST YOUR UNDERSTANDING

bought or brought?   We have _____ a castle haunted by a man who doesn't believe in ghosts.

off or of?   He had dived _____ the castle tower into the moat for a bet.

where or were?   No one had told him _____ the enormous and hungry Moaty Fish _____.

cloths or clothes?   Only his _____ survived.

of or off?   Now he has to haunt the place naked, which really cheeses him _____ .

Zelda, I've bought you trouble.

That's "brought", Steven, from "bring". "Bought" is from "buy" and means purchased. You don't mean that.

Oh. Do I have to take this back to the shop then?

ONE WORD OR TWO?

It can be difficult knowing whether you have to write one word or two on some occasions.

Always one word: **upstairs**
                        downstairs
                        cannot

Always two words: **a lot**
                        in front
                        in fact
                        all right

Sometimes one word; sometimes two words!! It all depends on which meaning you want.

ALMOST (= nearly) **ALL MOST** (= all of us).

I have **almost** finished.
We are **all most** grateful.

ALREADY (= before the expected time) **ALL READY** (= all of us)

We have **already** finished.
We are **all ready** for an emergency.

ALSO (= as well) **ALL SO** (= all of you)

He is **also** an artist.
You are **all so** kind.

ALWAYS (= at all times) **ALL WAYS** (= all the ways)

She is **always** happy.
All ways into the town were blocked by snow.

SOMETIMES (= now and again) **SOME TIMES**

I **sometimes** go fishing.
There are **some times** when I can't think of anything to do.

Just Mucking About

Time to relax! Those who like words and value-free information may be interested in homonyms and homographs.

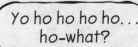

Yo ho ho ho ho. . .
ho-what?

HOMONYMS same spelling
same pronunciation
different meaning

For example, **box** is a homonym. It has at least two meanings:

a **box** of chocolates
to **box** in the boxing ring

Can you think of at least two meanings for each of these homonyms?

faint   **pen**   **plain**   **pine**   **match**

HOMOGRAPHS   same spelling
different pronunciation
different meaning

These are fascinating. See how you can say a homograph in two different ways. First say the word stressing the first syllable and then say the word stressing the second syllable.

project
PROject We are doing a *project* on transport through the ages.
proJECT You must *project* your voice to the back of the hall.

Say each of these words in two ways and see how they can mean two different things. (Look in the Answers section if you get stuck.)

entrance	ENtrance	enTRANCE
permit	PERmit	perMIT
conduct	CONduct	conDUCT
extract	EXtract	exTRACT
refuse	REfuse	reFUSE

COLIN'S CHALKBOARD CONCLUSIONS

Beware of the following:

1. Homophones: same sound, different spelling.
   Make sure you get the ~~write~~ right one.
2. Words which sound similar eg
   bought/brought, quiet/quite.
3. One word or two eg almost, all most.
   *Tip for 1 - 3: think about the meaning of the
   word rather than just the sound when you spell it.*
4. Homonyms: same spelling, same pronunciation,
   different meaning.
5. Homographs: same spelling, different
   pronunciation, different meaning.

4&5: A bit of a laugh - and happily no worries for spellers.

Do you want
a box?

Ooooh,
yes please.

ADDING BEGINNINGS

You have seen how words can be formed by adding endings to what are called "base words". In this section, we see how words can be formed by adding beginnings.

Shall we call them prefixes?

It really doesn't matter whether you call them prefixes or beginnings.

CLEVER TROUSERS

PREFIX THE LEGIONNAIRE ALWAYS CAME FIRST

WHOLE WORD PREFIXES

Sometimes prefixes can be whole words. Some whole word prefixes are: **out, over, under, up**.

Some quite ordinary base words are made into complicated-looking words when prefixes and suffixes are added. These words can look difficult to spell until you see how they are built up.

One of the longest words in the English language is said to be:

ANTIDISESTABLISHMENTARIANISM

It looks impossible to spell (or even say) until you see that it's simply the base word **ESTABLISH** with two prefixes (at the beginning) and three suffixes (at the end). Study the structure and you'll be able to spell it - and say it! - without difficulty.

ANTI DIS **ESTABLISH** MENT ARIAN ISM

If you learn how to spell prefixes and suffixes, you're more than halfway to spelling thousands and thousands of "combination" words.

Can you supply the missing letters? The prefix and the first
letter of the base word has been given to you to start you off.

OUT

outline	a drawing showing a general shape
outc_____	a person without home or friends
outb_____	a sudden explosion of anger
outl_____	a criminal, a person outside the law
outs_____	the edge of a town

OVER

oversleep	to sleep longer than planned
overc_____	to ask too high a price
overb_____	to lose one's footing and fall over
overf_____	to spill over
overb_____	over the side of a boat

UNDER

underground	below the ground
underw_____	clothes like pants and vests
underl_____	emphasise, draw a line under
underg_____	plants and bushes growing under trees
underh_____	deceitful, sly

UP

uproot	to pull up by the roots, to destroy
ups_____	to cause someone to be unhappy
upr_____	vertical, standing or sitting straight
upr_____	loud and noisy shouting
uph_____	tremendous change or disturbance

Don't worry if the word you make by adding a prefix to a base
word ends up with a double letter. That's how it should be!

over + react = overreact
under + rate = underrate

NEGATIVE PREFIXES

Some prefixes make their base words negative.

visible   **in**visible

There are four prefixes (**in**-, **un**-, **dis**-, **mis**-) which can reverse the meaning of base words in this way. The main problem is deciding which one you should use!

1. Remember too that sometimes when you add a negative prefix to a base word you will end up with a double letter in the "combination" word.

u**n** + **n**atural = u**nn**atural
di**s** + **s**atisfied = di**ss**atisfied
mi**s** + **s**pell = mi**ss**pell

2. Take care when you add in- to some words. Over the centuries, the n has changed to another letter to make the word easier to say.

These special forms need to be learned by heart. Here is a sample. Note other examples as you come across them.

noble   ignoble
legal   illegal
legible   illegible
literate   illiterate
patient   impatient
perfect   imperfect
possible   impossible
regular   irregular
relevant   irrelevant
responsible   irresponsible

You know most of these words already. So don't worry. You'll have to learn only a very few.

TEST YOUR WORD POWER
(and find the mystery word!)

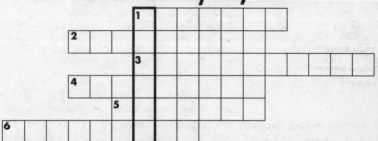

Use the correct negative prefix to form the opposite of:

1. OBEY
2. CORRECT
3. NECESSARY
4. BEHAVE
5. LEGAL
6. PATIENT

Did you find the mystery word?

Note how important prefixes can be:

NUMBER PREFIXES

Understanding the meaning of prefixes can help you spell some words, particularly ones with numbers in.

For instance: is it bipass or bypass, bicycle or bycycle?

Easy. A **by**pass goes by or around a town or city instead of going through it.
(by- means BY)
A **bi**cycle is a cycle with two wheels.
(bi- means TWO).

There are lots of other prefixes to do with numbers. Here are some of the most common ones.

uni- (one, single):	**uni**corn, **uni**cycle
mono- (one, single):	**mono**rail, **mono**syllable
bi- (two):	**bi**cycle, **bi**focals
tri- (three):	**tri**cycle, **tri**pod
quadr- (quad):	**quadr**uped, **quadr**uplets
deca- (ten):	**deca**de, **deci**mal
cent- (one hundred):	**cent**imetre, **cent**ury
mill- (one thousand):	**mill**imetre, **mill**ennium
poly- (many):	**poly**gon, **poly**syllable
omni- (all):	**omni**bus, **omni**vorous

Polygon   **Polly gone**

FIND THE WORDS

All these anagrams can be unscrambled to make words beginning with number prefixes.

> Find the prefix first and the rest will follow.

pdeeetnic: This creature has not really got a hundred feet.
dretint: Neptune has one of these three-pronged forks.
thlacendo: To win one of these you would have to get the highest overall score in ten different events.

Just Mucking About Again

Anagrams can be a bit of a laugh in general.

> "Dazle" is an anagram of Zelda, which is cool, because I'm a dazzling person.

> "Stevne" is an anagram of, er, Steven.

> Oh, come on Steven, you can do better than that. You really do make one v. tense.

> Why?

> Oh, I give up.

Can you make an anagram of your name?

And what anagram is this:

Segg

Answer: Scrambled "Eggs"

MORE PREFIXES

Most of the prefixes in the list below have come into our language from Latin and Greek (like the number prefixes we have just looked at). These prefixes can be very hard to spell but, on the other hand, once you HAVE learned how to spell them, you've often learned to spell the hardest part of lots of related words. And, in addition, you will have an important clue to their meaning. Look at the prefix chrono-. It comes from the Greek and means "time". Now a *chronic* illness is simply one that lasts for a long time (often for years). It is not necessarily a serious illness as so many people mistakenly suppose.

chrono- (time), **chron**ic, **chron**icle, **chron**ological, **chron**ology, **chron**ometer

ante- (before): **ante**natal
anti- (against): **anti**septic
auto- (self): **auto**biography
bene- (well): **bene**fit
chrono- (time): **chrono**logical
circum- (around): **circum**ference
contra- (against): **contra**dict
de- (from): **de**part
ex- (out of): **ex**pel
extra- (beyond): **extra**ordinary
fore- (before): **fore**cast
homo- (same): **homo**phone
inter- (between): **inter**national
male- (evil): **male**volent

micro- (small): **micro**scope
photo- (light): **photo**copy
per- (through): **per**forate
post- (after): **post**script
pre- (before): **pre**pare
psycho- (mind, soul): **psycho**logy
re- (again): **re**pay
semi- (half): **semi**-circle
sub- (under): **sub**marine
super- (above): **super**sonic
tele- (far off): **tele**vision
trans- (across): **trans**atlantic

REUNION

Draw a line to show which beginnings and endings could go together and then write the whole word in the space provided. The first one has been done for you.

1. anti	possible	1.	antidote
2. pre	colate	2.	_____
3. dis	phone	3.	_____
4. im	dote	4.	_____
5. sub	fer	5.	_____
6. per	natural	6.	_____
7. tele	appear	7.	_____
8. bene	pone	8.	_____
9. super	way	9.	_____
10. post	volent	10.	_____

So, if I think of that little lane leading to my house, does that make me a "psychopath"?

No, Steven, it makes you a microbrain.

THE SOUND ALIKE TWINS

Don't confuse ante- and anti-. They sound alike but they are spelled differently.

If you know what they mean, you will always know which you need.

ante means **before**

Expectant mothers attend an *antenatal* clinic *before* their babies are born.

ante + natal = before + birth

anti means **against**

Motorists put *antifreeze* in their car radiators.

anti + freeze = against + freezing

Hello, I'm Aunty Natal.

Antenatal   **Anti-Natal**   **Aunty Natal**

IDENTIFY THE MISSING LETTERS

See if the prefix means
before (ante)
or against (anti).

ant__clockwise	in the opposite direction to the way the hands of a clock go round
ant__septic	kills microbes
ant__room	a waiting room outside a larger room
ant__dote	a medicine which stops the effects of poison
ant__cedents	ancestors
ant__diluvian	so outdated it could have happened before the Biblical flood
ant__perspirant	this stops perspiration
ant__pathy	a strong feeling of dislike
ant__podes	a place on the opposite side of the world to where you are
ant__biotic	medicine which works by killing the germs causing the illness

That's all you need to know about prefixes.

I hope that's not too much
of an anti-climax.

COLIN'S CHALKBOARD CONCLUSIONS

You can add a prefix, or two,
to make a new word.

1. Learn the common prefixes.

2. Know what they mean.

Then you'll be more likely to spell the
longer word accurately.

They say that pre-vention is better than cure.
That is, doing things before the problem arises
is a good idea. I suppose that . . . if I were to
mend your car before a problem arose. . .

That would be a "pre-fix".

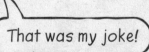

That was my joke!

Just Mucking About Again

Let's talk about spoonerisms.

> SPOONERISM (noun) - the swapping round of the first letters or sounds of a group of words to create a funny effect. e.g. a well-boiled icicle (a well-oiled bicycle).

> That's really called METATHESIS, or changing sounds (META + THESIS).

CLEVER TROUSERS

Rev. Dr William Archibald Spooner (1844-1930) was a very clever man and warden of New College, Oxford. He didn't MEAN to muddle so many words and phrases when he spoke to his students but unfortunately he became so well known for it that such verbal muddles became named after him. In 1879 he announced the next hymn as "Kinquering Congs their titles take." Do you think the congregation sang the right words after this?

A half-formed wish.   **A half-warmed fish.**

What do you think Dr Spooner MEANT to say instead of these spoonerisms?

1. The Lord is a shoving leopard.

2. You have hissed all my mystery lectures.

3. You have tasted two whole worms.

4. Let us drink to the queer old Dean.

5. He's a boiled sprat.

Keep your ears open for spoonerisms. They usually happen in the heat of the moment. Perhaps someone will yell at you to "Doze the claw!" or "Fipe your wheat!" You probably muddled words like "carpark" when you were a child or have family spoonerisms like "chish and fips".

Once you start deliberately swapping sounds around, it gets infectious: drairhesser, prying fan, bustdin, a clicking tock . . .

Can you think of any more?

SILENT LETTERS

Did you know that over half the letters of the alphabet can be used silently in words?

Here are just three examples:

You don't hear the b in this word:

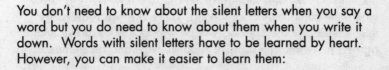

You don't hear the h in this word:

You don't hear the s in this word:

You don't need to know about the silent letters when you say a word but you do need to know about them when you write it down. Words with silent letters have to be learned by heart. However, you can make it easier to learn them:

If you think of other words in the same family where the silent letter *is* pronounced (si**g**n and si**g**nature, for example).

If you learn silent letter words in letter groups (all the silent b words together and so on).

If you can devise funny ways to remember the hard words (don't i**g**nore a **g**nu).

If you learn as much about the background of the words as you can (**sc**ience comes from Latin **sc**ire – to know).

Some letters that are silent in particular words today used to be voiced (that is, pronounced) years and years ago.

Take the word **knight**, for example. We pronounce it *nite*. Geoffrey Chaucer, who lived 600 years ago, would have pronounced the k at the beginning and would have had a go at pronouncing the gh as well. He would have said *ker-nikt*. (Say it that way to yourself when you are spelling it if it helps.)

You probably think it's strange that letters that became silent weren't dropped. You may think it even stranger that silent letters were added to some perfectly good words that didn't need them and never had needed them. The words **doute** and **dette** had a silent b added just to show that they came from the Latin words "dubitum" and "dubitare". That's how **doubt** and **debt** became such tricky words to spell.

Printers and dictionary makers did a lot of this kind of "tidying up" of the language as consistency in spelling became more and more important.

Spelling has become standardised and we now have to know where the silent letters are lurking. There are two reasons for this. If we don't our spelling will be wrong, OK? Just live with it, right? We'll look stupid, have rubbish lives, and be shunned.

Also, we do have something to thank silent letters for. Thanks to them, we know the meaning of words which would be different without them.

We know that **knit** doesn't mean **nit**.
We know that **aisle** is different from **isle**.
We know that **reign** is not the same thing as **rain** or **rein**.

And see opposite for an entirely true story about all this. Only the facts have been changed.

So, you kneed to now them. Rats. Need to know them. Let's have a look...

Spelling Mistakes
that Changed the Course of History, part 912

THE ASSASSIN RECEIVED HIS ORDERS FROM THE EVIL CARDINAL.

THIS WAS NO ORDINARY JOB.

EVIL CARDINAL

THROUGH THE BACK STREETS HE SLIPPED.

HE SPIED HIS PREY.

BENEATH HIS CAPE HE ASSEMBLED HIS EQUIPMENT.

MENACINGLY HE MOVED THROUGH THE CROWD TOWARDS THE KING.

HE SPRANG ON TO THE STAGE.

FASTER AND FASTER HE MOVED, CLOSER AND CLOSER HE CAME, UNTIL...

HE WAS LATER GIVEN A SMALL REWARD.

You must bring an end to the King's rain Tonight.

Here are some of the main groups.

Silent **b** words

The letter b, printed in bold type, is silent in the words below.

Say the words aloud without voicing the silent b but noticing that it is there.

lam**b**
bom**b**
crum**b**
dum**b**, dum**b**founded
clim**b**, clim**b**er
succum**b**

You often find silent b after m.

And remember silent b in: de**b**t dou**b**t su**b**tle

Silent **c** words

Look out for **sc** in words where the c is silent. Here are a few. There are lots of others. If you had only ever heard the words said and never seen them written down, you wouldn't know they each had a letter c in them.

s**c**enery   fas**c**inate
s**c**ent   des**c**endant
dis**c**iple

I sent you some perfume –
it must have got lost in the post.
I scent a lame excuse.

DEFUSE THE SILENT BOMB

Can you unjumble these words? Like "bomb" they all end in a silent "b". And to help you concentrate, we might just have wired this book up to a silent bomb that will go off if you don't solve them all within 60 seconds starting from ... NOW.

tbhmu   a digit on the hand

bmto   a burial place

mlbi   a jointed part of the body,

               such as an arm or leg

OVER TO YOU!

Can you spell these words?

_ _ _ _ _ _ _ _

_ _ _ _ _

_ _ _ _ _

Numb hands   **Numb feet**   **Numbskull**

Silent g words

Say these words aloud, being careful not to voice the silent g.

gnaw si**g**n **g**nat si**g**npost **g**nash rei**g**n
gnarled forei**g**n **g**nome desi**g**n **g**nu campai**g**n

The combination **gn** is one to look out for, especially if you're trying to find a word in the dictionary that sounds as if it should start with n.

Sometimes other words in the same word family help, as we've said already:

si**g**n but sig-nal and sig-nature.

Some people find it helpful to *say* the g when learning to spell a silent g word:

The gnome gnawed a gnu. (The nome nawed a nu).
The ger-nome ger-nawed a ger-nu.

Silent gh words

There are lots of gh words.

some au**gh** ones:
dau**gh**ter cau**gh**t nau**gh**ty

some ei**gh** ones:
ei**gh**t wei**gh** nei**gh**bour slei**gh**

i**gh** words are far more interesting:

li**gh**t li**gh**thouse ni**gh**t ni**gh**tmare si**gh**t fi**gh**t ri**gh**t

 But the words that are the MOST interesting are ough ones. See how each of these words has a different **ough** sound!

enou**gh** (-uff) althou**gh** (-o) cou**gh** (-off) bou**gh** (-ow)
throu**gh** (-oo) bou**gh**t (-ort)

BRAIN CELL QUESTION!

Can you think of four more words spelled **-ought** that rhyme with bought?

1. _____
2. _____
3. _____
4. _____

G-WHIZZ

Match up the right definition with these silent g words.

You're allowed to use a dictionary!

a) gnocchi   1) rod on a sundial that casts the shadow

b) gnomon   2) snarl or growl

c) gnathic   3) small dumplings in a sauce

d) gnar   4) relating to the jaws

That top puzzle's difficult, isn't it. I thought I ought to do it, but however much I fought, my efforts came to nought.

It might be easier than you think, idiot.

Silent h words

Read these words. Be careful not to pronounce the h!

heir, **h**eiress, **h**eirloom
honest, **h**onesty
hour
honour
r**h**inoceros
r**h**yme
ex**h**ibit
ve**h**icle
catar**h**
antirr**h**inum

and Jo**h**n which comes from the Latin Johannes
(pronounced Jo-hann-us).

Silent k words

Steven, I'll give you £5 if you
can say five words with a
silent "k" before I say knife.

I won't know any.
I haven't got the knack
for that sort of thing.
I just get my knickers
knitted in a knot.

Five! Well done – but I'm afraid I've
already said knife – so you're
knocked out of the competition!

Silent m words

Mnemonic (pronounced NEM-ON-ICK) begins with a silent m
but I'll tell you about mnemonics in the next chapter.

MISSING LETTERS

Can you complete these words?

ch – – –   several musical notes
                played together
gh – – – – –   small green cucumber
                usually pickled
kh – – –   colour of army uniforms
rh – – – – –   plant with thick juicy
                stems you can eat

No, I said today you should wear your *khaki* uniform.

The Importance of Spelling in Literature, part 96

... They travelled by night
to avoid detection ...

... They travelled by knight
to avoid detection ...

Silent n words

These silent n words need watching. Look at the two lists below. In the left-hand list, the n is silent in all the words. In the right-hand list, where suffixes have been added, the n is voiced.

Shhh!   *Say it!*

condemn   condem-nation
solemn   solem-nity
damn   dam-nation
autumn   autum-nal
hymn   hym-nal

Silent p words

Notice:
ras**p**berry
cu**p**board
cor**p**s
recei**p**t

and all the words we get from Greek beginning with **p**n, **p**s, **p**t.

The p is not voiced in these words.

pneumonia
pneumatic
psalm
psychology
ptarmigan
pterodactyl

What am I? Please unjumble me:

Answer: column

BRAINBOX OF THE UNIVERSE QUIZ

ps - - - - nym   (an assumed name, a pen name)
ps - - - - sis   (an itchy disease of the skin)

Pterodactyl

Terror Daryl

Silent s words

aisle   isle   island

Both isle and island come from an old English word 'iland' or 'igland'. Some clever people *added* a silent s to both words because they thought the words came from the Latin 'insula'. Now we're stuck with the results of this mistaken identity.

Did anyone notice that **ai**sle has two silent letters?

Silent t words

There are two ways of saying OFTEN. How do you say it?

You can say OFF-EN (silent t).
You can say OFF-TEN (voiced t).

Both ways are correct but you must always spell the word OFTEN.

Here are some -stle words.

castle
trestle
hustle and bustle
mistletoe

And don't forget the MORTGAGE!

Here are some -sten words.

moisten
fasten
listen
christen

The Importance of Spelling in Geography, part 29

When you write about

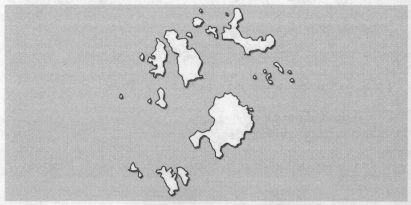

The Scilly Isles

the Scilly Isles, a group of remote and beautiful islands off the coast of Cornwall, it is important not to write about

The Silly Aisles

the Silly Aisles, which are in the National Cathedral of Gagaland, designed by Jack El-Loco in 1857.

Silent U words

I wish you were silent!

lots of words begin with **gu**.

For example, think of g**u**ide and g**u**ardian and g**u**est.

Try the test opposite to see how many you know.

And don't forget these!
bisc**u**it, b**u**oy, b**u**ilding

And remember that there is British English and North American English.

hono**u**r	honor
splendo**u**r	splendor
labo**u**r	labor
humo**u**r	humor
colo**u**r	color

And you always have u after q. This is easy to remember.

If there's a Q, U always joins at the back.

Silent W words

Do you know these silent w words?

wren	**w**rist
write	**w**rinkle
wrap	**w**rong

SILENT U TEST:

gu_____   opposite of innocent

gu_____   formal promise

gu_____   beheading machine

gu_____   musical instrument

We guarantee it won't actually cut your head off - or your money back!

MAGICIANS' SUPPLIES

SILENT W CROSSWORD

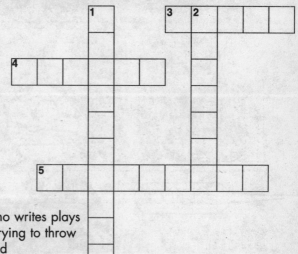

Down
1. A person who writes plays
2. To fight by trying to throw to the ground

Across
3. A weapon with a long steel blade
4. A circle of flowers and leaves
5. Destruction of a ship at sea

COLiN'S CHALKBOARD CONCLUSIONS

SILENT LETTERS

You have to know about silent letters because:

1. Sometimes, if you leave them out, you change the meaning of the word completely.
2. Anyway, whether you think they're a good idea or not, the proper spelling of lots of words involves silent letters, and if you don't get them right you'll look stupid and generally lose marks in life.
3. So, notice them when you see them written down; invent any way you can that'll help you remember.

Silent C!

MNEMONICS

Can we have MNEMONICS now?
What ARE they?

A mnemonic is a memory trick, anything that helps you to remember dates, or spellings, or scientific facts or anything else that is important to you.

For example, as a way of remembering the points of the compass (North, East, South and West) and where they are, you can remember "**N**ever **E**at **S**oggy **W**heat", and that will remind you that the initial letters are NESW. These go clockwise around the compass like this:

The good news is that you can use mnemonics for loads of things. We'll get to the spelling ones in a moment, but let's just muck about with some others first. You may know some of these already.

COLOURS OF THE RAINBOW MNEMONIC

Richard **O**f **Y**ork **G**ave **B**attle **I**n **V**ain

R red
O orange
Y yellow
G green
B blue
I indigo
V violet

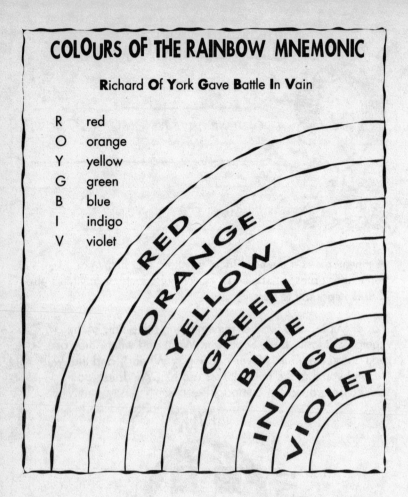

Or: **R**emember **O**nly **Y**oung **G**irls **B**elieve **I**n **V**ampires

Or: **R**ely **O**n **Y**our **G**reen **B**icycle **I**n **V**ietnam!

Or you can remember that there was an American millionaire who called himself Roy G. Biv.

It doesn't matter which sentence you remember as long as it works. Mnemonics are meant to *help* you remember. Choose whichever sentence you like best or make another one up if you prefer.

LINES ON A MUSICAL STAVE MNEMONIC

Every Good Boy Deserves Favours

E G B D F

HISTORICAL DATE MNEMONIC

In fourteen hundred and ninety-two
Columbus sailed the ocean blue.

And discovered the West Indies.

SOPHIE SMARTIPANTS

Thank you, Sophie. That's splendid. That's quite enough for
now. We'll look at some spelling mnemonics in the next
section. Ready?

SPELLING MNEMONICS

There's one very well known one which you may know too. (Unfortunately, most people know only the first two lines).

IE/EI MNEMONIC

Put I before E
except after C
or when sounded like A
as in neighbour or weigh

Let's look at some examples to see how well the rule works.

IE	EI after C	EI sounding like A
priest, friend,	ceiling, receive,	neighbour, weigh,
field, shield,	receipt, deceive,	eight, weight,
chief, thief,	perceive	freight, reign,
belief, relief,		rein, vein,
niece, piece,		their, heir
fierce, pierce,		
relieve, grieve,		
reprieve, achieve,		
shriek, siege,		
view, review,		
hygiene		

81

That's a fantastic rule. Are there lots of exceptions?

Well, no. There really aren't many. Here are the most important ones.

1. These words are EI when you would expect them to be IE:

counterf**ei**t h**ei**fer **ei**ther s**ei**ze l**ei**sure
n**ei**ther w**ei**rd sover**ei**gn h**ei**ght for**ei**gn

2. Names don't follow this rule and so you have Sh**ei**la, D**ei**rdre, N**ei**l and K**ei**th.

The IE/EI rule is really useful provided that you remember the last two lines.

If you don't remember this one, you really could look STUPID.

Trade's slow again today.

Read the IE/EI mnemonic again and see how you get on with the basic MOT.

Just apply the rule.
No exceptions here.

BASIC MOT
ie or ei?

1. Conc – – t
2. Bel – – ve
3. R – – ndeer
4. Misch – – f
5. V – – l

The words in the advanced MOT are longer but the rule is just the same. One exception has been included to keep you on your toes!

ADVANCED MOT
ie or ei?

1. Ach – – vement
2. Misch – – vous
3. Handkerch – – f
4. B – – ge
5. H – – rloom
6. Gr – – vance
7. Surv – – llance
8. For – – gn
9. Interv – – w
10. Conc – – ve

Here are a few more mnemonics you may find useful.

Explanation or **explaination?**
Remember there's a **plan** in ex**plan**ation.

Here or **hear** (when you mean "listen")?
You h**ear** with your **ear**.

Friend or **freind?**

That's the **end** of my fri**end**!

Lonely or **lonley?**
One person can be l**one**ly

Lose or **loose** (when you mean 'wobbly')?
L**oo**k at my l**oo**se t**oo**th.

Necessary, neccessary, neccesary, or **necesary?**
You need **one c**ollar and **a pair of s**ocks.

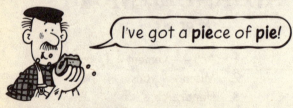

I've got a **pie**ce of **pie**!

Secertary or **secretary?**
A **secret**ary can keep a **secret**.

Separate or **seperate?**
There's **a rat** in sep **a rat** e.

Stationery or **stationary** (when you mean 'not moving')?
A station**ary** c**ar**.

You can have fun with acrostic sentences as well. This is where each letter is used to begin a word in a sentence.

Never	**N**obody
Ever	**E**ver
Combine	**C**omes
Egg	**E**very
Sandwiches	**S**ingle
Sardines	**S**unday
And	**A**nd
Raspberry	**R**emembers
Yoghurt	**Y**ou.

Have a go yourself at making an acrostic sentence for "necessary".

N _____

E _____

C _____

E _____

S _____

S _____

A _____

R _____

Y _____

Nightly **E**xtra **C**orn **E**nsures **S**teven's **S**tumpy **A**rms **R**emain **Y**ellow.

Taking words apart

Another useful way of remembering how to spell a word is to take it apart and to be aware of how the parts fit together.

Mis + spell = mi**ss**pell (double s)
un + necessary = u**nn**ecessary (double n)
dis + appear = di**s**appear (single s)
real + ly = rea**ll**y (double l)
sincere + ly = sincer**e**ly (keep the e)

A word like **criticism** can look difficult to spell. It's much less formidable (for+mid+able) when you see that it's just critic + ism.

Word families

Use your knowledge of word families to help you with other words in the same family.

Signature will help you with **sign**.
Govern will help you with **govern**ment.
Adapt**ation** will help you with adapt**able**.
Mean will help you with **mean**t.
Gradual will help you with **gradual**ly.
Ab**sen**t will help you with ab**sen**ce.

Look carefully

Take a long hard look at words you are trying to learn. Notice anything really odd about them that may stick in your mind.

Notice the -wkw- in a**wkw**ard.
Notice the -hth- in eig**hth**.
Notice that **unusu**al has three **u**s.
Notice words like f**acetiou**s that have all five vowels in the right order.

Enjoy these oddities and spelling will be fun too.

Say the words carefully

Make sure you say words carefully. Some people misspell words because they say them wrongly.

Make sure you say:

It's the correct pro-nun-ciation you need, innit?

arctic	not artic
Antarctic	not Antartic
burglar two syllables,	not burgular
chimney	not chimley
chocolate three syllables,	not choclate
equipment	not equiptment
expedition	not experdition
February	not Febuary
government	not goverment
gradually	not gradully
handkerchief	not hankerchief
hundred two syllables,	not hundered
information	not imformation
interesting four syllables,	not intresting
library	not libary
mischievous three syllables,	not mischievious
nephew pronounced "neffew",	not nevew
packed lunch	not pack lunch
pantomime	not pantomine
perhaps	not prehaps
probably	not propably or proballly
recognise or **recognize**	not reconise or reconize
sandwich	not sanwich
secretary	not secertary
surprise	not suprise
twelfth	not twelth
umbrella	not umberella
vegetable four syllables,	not vegtable
veterinary five syllables,	not vetinary

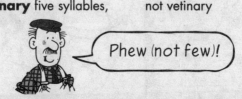

Phew (not few)!

Extra *e*

Do you know why you have to keep the e in the words below?

Notice + able	notic**e**able
Pronounce + able	pronounc**e**able
Service + able	servic**e**able
Change + able	chang**e**able
Venge + ance	veng**e**ance
Courage + ous	courag**e**ous

If you know about soft and hard c and g, it all makes sense and it is easier to remember.

The letter c has two sounds: either soft s or hard k.
The letter g has two sounds: either soft j or hard g.
The letters c and g are usually hard in front of a, o, u: cat, cot, cut; gap, got, gun.

They are usually soft in front of e, i, y: cell, cider, cycle; germ, ginger, gym.

By keeping the e in words like notic**e**able and courag**e**ous, you keep the c and g soft.

Got that, Steven? So does -e make a letter hard or soft?

I love Mr Soft-ee!

Soft and hard c
WORDSEARCH

Find these words in the wordsearch square:

cavity	compass	cider	coin
century	cast	coast	circle
certain	cycle		

Words may be arranged vertically, horizontally or diagonally and may be written forwards or backwards. The same letter can be used more than once.

```
C  O  A  S  T  Z  R  A
E  A  D  J  V  E  B  C
N  L  V  C  D  U  E  O
T  R  C  I  N  R  L  M
U  P  C  R  T  M  C  P
R  O  G  A  I  Y  Y  A
Y  S  I  H  S  C  C  S
T  N  I  O  C  T  R  S
```

How many "soft c" words did you find?
How many "hard c" words did you find?

Without looking at the list of words that you need to say carefully (on page 87) see if you can complete these words from memory.

WHICH LETTERS ARE MISSING?

1. sec – – tary
2. vet – – inary
3. han – kerchief
4. Feb – uary
5. pro – ably

Extra k

picnic + ing = picnicking

Now that you know about soft and hard c, can you work out why we have to add a k to "picnicking"?

The answer is that without the k, "cing" would sound like "sing" as it does in the word "icing".

Do these word sums, putting in the extra k where it is needed.

Remember that c is soft
(sounds like s)
in front of e, i, y.

TEST YOUR SKILL

1. panic + s   _____
2. panic + y   _____
3. mimic + ing   _____
4. mimic + ed   _____
5. mimic + ry   _____
6. picnic + er   _____
7. picnic + ed   _____
8. picnic + s   _____

Steven has NOT read this section very carefully.

Will you mark his spelling test for him and tell him his score?

(Would you be kind enough to write his corrections for him beside any words he has got wrong?)

Steven S. Monster

1 Receive
2 Separate
3 Sincerley
4 Freind
5 Lonley
6 Panicks
7 Intrested
8 Realy
9 Necessary
10 Couragous

Score: /10

Comment:

Marker's initials:

Well, if you're so clever, can you spell these words:

Steven, don't you think it's a bit easy given that you've written them out?

Pronounceable
Handkerchief
Signature
Unnecessary
Expedition

COLIN'S CHALKBOARD CONCLUSIONS

1. Put i before e except after c. or when sounded like a, as in neighbour and weigh. (Only a few exceptions).

2. Think of your own silly sentences for tricky words (like, 'a secretary can keep a secret').

3. Take words apart (separating prefixes and suffixes) to see how the word is made up).

4. If you need a soft c or g, you'll probably need an -e to follow them.

5. Add k to c to make it hard.

Use as many mnemonics as you like to remember those tricky spellings. Do you know about Mnemonics?

Can't remember him.

USEFUL LISTS
TRICKY WORDS

Most people will find these words difficult to spell. Remember they are here when you want to use them. Best of all, learn them by heart as soon as you can.

absolutely
across
address
afraid
among
amount
annoy
any
apology
argument
autumn

beautiful
because
before
broken
burglar
business

character
chocolate
college
completely

definitely
describe
description
different
difficult

embarrass
especially
excellent
except
excitement
exercise
exhausted
explanation
extraordinary

family

fascinating
favourite
finish
fortunately
frightened

gradually
grateful
guess

heard
honestly
horrible
humorous

immediately
information
innocent
intelligent
interesting
invisible

jealous

library
luxury

mention
mischievous
moment

necessary
neighbour

obedient
occasionally
opinion
opportunity

paid
parent
passenger
perhaps

pleasant
possible
possibly
probably

realise (-ize)
really
recent
recognise (-ize)
referee
responsible
ridiculous

sandwich
scissors
separate
separately
severely
similar
sincerely
soldier
sometimes
speech
suggest
suppose
surely
surprise

tired
tomorrow

until
useful
usually

valuable
vegetable
vehicle

woman
women
woollen

NUMBERS

When you write stories, poems, plays and letters, you will generally write numbers in words instead of figures - and some are quite tricky to spell. There is no rule for these, you just have to learn them. Take particular care with these numbers:

twelve	second
fourteen	fifth
fifteen	eighth
nineteen	ninth
forty	twelfth
ninety-nine	fifteenth
one hundred	twentieth

The only numbers that need hyphens are combination numbers up to 99.

So. You've read the book. You've done the tests. Are you a spelling genius?

Well, if you're normal, probably not quite yet. But we've got four tips to help you on your way:

Make yourself a spelling notebook.
Writing any words you seem to use a lot in a handy book can save you time when you're looking them up and help you learn them.

Find a good dictionary.
Make sure you use a dictionary which is well laid out and easy to understand - they're not all the same!

Always check your work.
Read through everything you write to make sure you haven't made any careless mistakes. Check the spelling of any words that you're not sure of.

And . . . take pride in what you do.
Make everything that you write as good as you can. Spelling is a bit like life; most of it's down to you. So good luck, and may the spelling force be with you!

ANSWERS

(page numbers are in brackets)

MORE THAN ONE
Basic MOT (19) 1. books,
2. wishes, 3. teachers, 4. pens,
5. glasses.
Advanced MOT (19)
1. winches, 2. ruminants,
3. blemishes, 4. mnemonics
5. zygoranismagicianisticalists.
Basic MOT (22) 1. flies,
2. toys, 3. bullies, 4. holidays,
5. donkeys, 6. berries, 7. spies,
8. stories, 9. valleys, 10. ponies.
Advanced MOT (23)
1. essays, 2. fantasies,
3. opportunities, 4. factories,
5. volleys, 6. universities,
7. qualities, 8. pulleys,
9. responsibilities, 10. convoys.
Odd One Out (25) shelf (shelves)
Find the Mystery Word (26)
The mystery word is *sheaves* 1.
ladies, 2. witches, 3. women,
4. potatoes, 5. knives,
6. children, 7. sopranos.

ADDING ENDINGS
Vital Missing Letter (30)
1. y, 2. i, 3. y, 4. i, 5. i.
Advanced MOT (31) 1. i,
2. i, 3. y, 4. i, 5. y, 6. i, 7. y,
8. i, 9. i, 10. i.
Sophie's Test (32) 1. ✓,
2. careless, 3. ✓, 4. sincerely,
5. safety.
Henry VIII's letter (33)
writing, lonely, definitely,
hoping, grateful, sincerely.

HOMOPHONES
Missing partners (38)
whole, tale, thrown, would,
son, *son, thrown, for, whole,
tale, would,* profit, isle, meddle,
hymn, sealing.
Missing pairs (39) male/mail
die/dye, heel/heal, alter/altar.
Zandra's letter (40)
1. deer/dear, 2. wood/would,
3. yew/you, 4. hole/whole,
5. weak/week, 6. beech/beach,
7. grate/great, 8. right/write
9. yew/you, 10. reed/read.
Missing letters (40) hoarse,
some, meat, allowed, cheque.
Testing, Testing (41)
1. who's, 2. hear, 3. too/to/two
4. it's, 5. know/no.
Test Your Understanding
(43) bought, where, were,

clothes, off.
Homographs (45)
ENtrance way in,
enTRANCE bewitch, delight,
PERmit written permission,
perMIT allow,
CONduct behaviour,
conDUCT lead,
EXtract small part from whole,
exTRACT draw out,
REfuse rubbish,
reFUSE say no.

ADDING BEGINNINGS
Whole word prefixes (49)
OUT
outcast, outburst, outlaw,
outskirts.
OVER
overcharge, overbalance,
overflow, overboard.
UNDER
underwear, underline,
undergrowth, underhand
UP
upset, upright, uproar, upheaval.
Test Your Word Power (51)
1. disobey, 2. incorrect,
3. unnecessary, 4. misbehave,
5. illegal, 6. impatient
The mystery word is *double.*
Find the words (53)
centipede, trident, decathlon.
Reunion (55) 2. prefer,
3. disappear, 4. impossible,
5. subway, 6. percolate,
7. telephone, 8. benevolent,
9. supernatural, 10. postpone.
Identify the missing letters
(57) anticlockwise, antiseptic,
anteroom, antidote,
antecedents, antediluvian,
antiperspirant, antipathy,
antipodes, antibiotic.
Spoonerisms (60) 1. The
Lord is a loving shepherd.
2. You have missed all my
history lectures. 3. You have wasted two whole
terms. 3. Let us drink to the
dear old Queen. 4. He's a
spoiled brat.

SILENT LETTERS
Defuse the Silent Bomb
(65) thumb, tomb, limb.
Over to You (65) scissors,
scythe, muscle.

Brain cell question (67)
(more answers possible) sought,
fought, brought, wrought.
G-Whizz
(67) a=3, b=1, c=4, d=2.
Missing Letters (69)
chord, gherkin, khaki, rhubarb.
Brainbox of the Universe
(71) pseudonym, psoriasis.
Silent U Test (75) guilty,
guarantee, guillotine, guitar.
Silent W Crossword (75)
Down 1. playwright,
2. wrestle.
Across 3. sword, 4. wreath,
5. shipwreck.

MNEMONICS
Basic MOT (83) 1. conceit,
2. believe, 3. reindeer,
4. mischief, 5. veil.
Advanced MOT (83)
1. achievement, 2. mischievous,
3. handkerchief, 4. beige,
5. heirloom, 6. grievance,
7. surveillance, 8. foreign,
9. interview, 10. conceive.
Wordsearch (89)
5 soft c words, 5 hard c words.

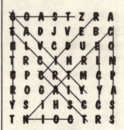

Which letters are missing
(89) 1. secretary, 2. veterinary,
3. handkerchief, 4. February,
5. probably.
Test your skills (90)
1. panics, 2. panicky,
3. mimicking, 4. mimicked,
5. mimicry, 6. picnicker,
7. picnicked, 8. picnics.
Steven's Spelling Test (91)
1. ✓, 2. ✓, 3. sincerely,
4. friend, 5. lonely, 6. panics,
7. interested, 8. really, 9. ✓,
10. courageous.
Score: 3/10